DK Eyewonder

Ancient Rome

LONDON, NEW YORK,
MELBOURNE, MUNICH, and DELHI

Written and edited by Lorrie Mack
Designed by Clare Shedden
Additional design Andrew Nash

Art director Rachael Foster
Publishing manager Bridget Giles
Picture researcher Liz Moore
Production editor Sean Daly
Production controller Pip Tinsley
Jacket designer Natalie Godwin
Jacket editor Mariza O'Keefe

Consultant Angus Konstam

First published in Great Britain in 2009 by
Dorling Kindersley Limited
80 Strand, London WC2R 0RL

Printed and bound by Star Standard, Singapore

Discover more at
www.dk.com

Contents

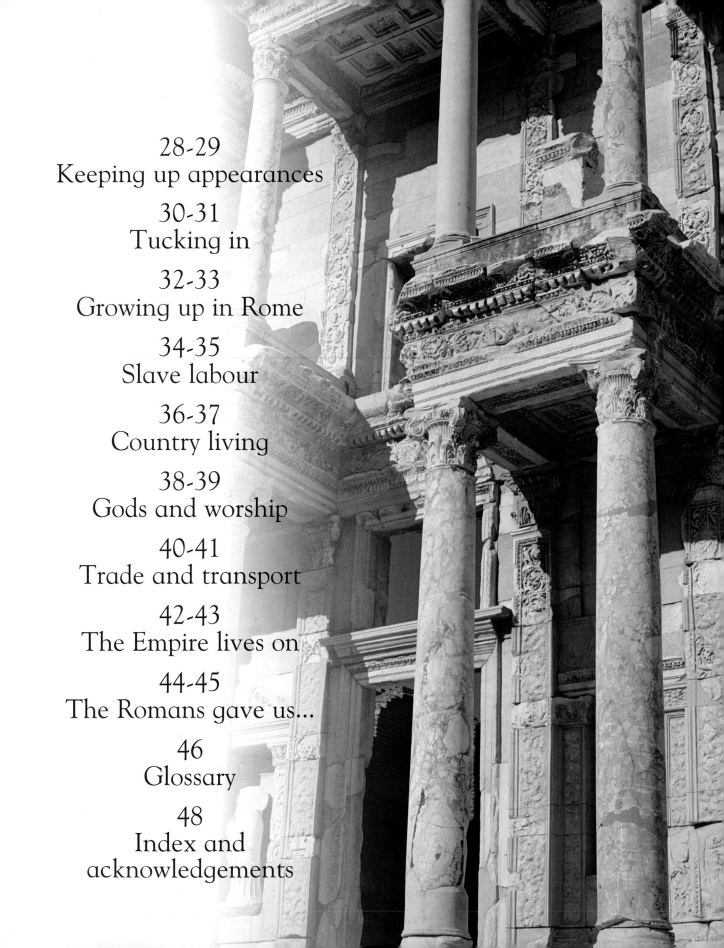

Welcome to ancient Rome

According to myth, Rome was founded by Romulus and Remus, twin sons of war god Mars. They built a great city, but in the end, they quarrelled, and Romulus killed Remus. Rome is named after Romulus.

Two brothers

When they were born, Romulus and Remus were left on the banks of the Tiber to die. They were found by a she-wolf, who fed them until a shepherd came to their rescue and raised them as his own.

The last king

Early Rome was ruled by kings. In 509BCE, the last king, called Tarquin the Proud (above), was banished. Rome then became a republic – a place where power is held by the people, or by the representatives they vote for.

Eternal city

Built on seven hills near the River Tiber, Rome was the biggest city in the ancient world, and it is still a thriving capital city thousands of years later.

Life at the top

During the Republic, Rome was governed by a group of noblemen called the Senate, led by two consuls. They shared the job of governing, and were elected every year. Later Rome was ruled by emperors (*see* pages 18-19).

Some citizens had bronze copies made of their citizenship documents.

Who's who?

People in ancient Rome were either citizens, who were free and could vote, or slaves, who were owned by other people (*see* pages 34-35). To be a citizen you had to appear on the official census.

Census-taking shown on a stone relief from the Temple of Neptune in Rome

Good neighbours

Rome was heavily influenced by two of its neighbours – the Greeks and the Etruscans. Both were older cultures that produced great artists, architects, and scholars. Greek and Etruscan religion also affected Roman beliefs.

Etruscan musicians shown on a 5th-century tomb fresco

Grand Roman buildings reflect the style of Greece. This is the Parthenon, near Athens.

CONQUER IN STYLE

Roman armies were large and powerful, but their strength was not always needed. Sometimes, when soldiers arrived in a new land, the natives were so impressed with their style, their comforts, and their efficiency that they were quite happy to be ruled by them. In fact, Rome's brilliant branding was often as effective as its military might.

Soldiers crossed large bodies of water in galley warships. These were powered by both sails and oars. Slaves did all the rowing.

The Roman Empire, divided into provinces (Names of modern countries in brackets)

Hadrian's Wall

Britannia (Britain)

Gaul (France)

The Alps

Hispania (Spain)

Mediterranean Sea

Carthage

AFRICA

Win and defend
Once they conquered foreign lands, Roman soldiers stayed to guard them. Each soldier was expected to serve the Empire for about 25 years.

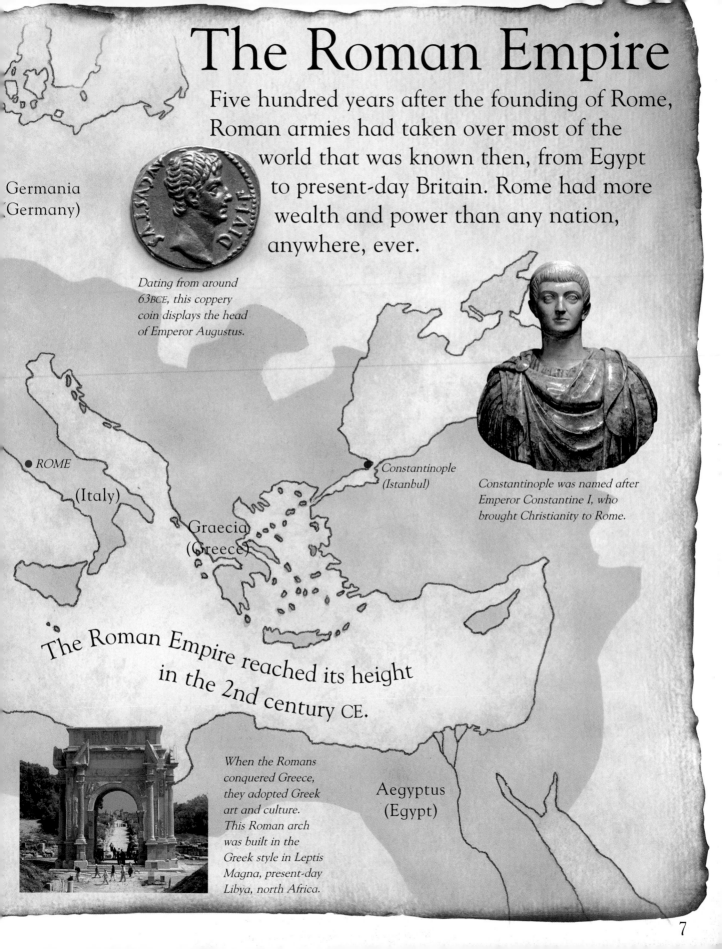

The Roman Empire

Five hundred years after the founding of Rome, Roman armies had taken over most of the world that was known then, from Egypt to present-day Britain. Rome had more wealth and power than any nation, anywhere, ever.

Germania (Germany)

Dating from around 63BCE, this coppery coin displays the head of Emperor Augustus.

ROME (Italy)

Graecia (Greece)

Constantinople (Istanbul)

Constantinople was named after Emperor Constantine I, who brought Christianity to Rome.

The Roman Empire reached its height in the 2nd century CE.

When the Romans conquered Greece, they adopted Greek art and culture. This Roman arch was built in the Greek style in Leptis Magna, present-day Libya, north Africa.

Aegyptus (Egypt)

The Empire strikes out!

In their struggle to expand and defend their Empire, the Romans fought huge, bloody battles and short skirmishes (small battles). Sometimes they lost, but much more often, they were victorious.

At one time, there were about 375,000 men in the Roman army.

Leading every unit was a man carrying the army's standard, or symbol – the eagle. It represented Rome's power.

Carved in stone
The Picts carved these strange stone slabs over many centuries. They are the only visual record we have of Pictish culture.

Computer reconstruction of Hadrian's Wall

Take your Pict
The Romans invaded Britain, but they could not control the Caledonians (Picts), an ancient tribe in the north – what is now Scotland. In the second century CE, the Roman Emperor Hadrian built an enormous wall to keep them out and to mark the Empire's boundary. Parts of it are still standing.

The fight for Gaul

From 58 to 52BCE, the Romans fought to control Gaul (modern-day France). They succeeded spectacularly because Augustus Caesar had many friends in Gaul. Also, many Gallic soldiers served in his legions, and several Gallic tribes asked for his help in their battles with other Gallic tribes.

The Gallic leader Vercingetorix surrendering to Caesar.

Battle of Arausio

Rome was not always triumphant. This earlier action in Gaul in 105BCE resulted in the total defeat of Rome by the Cimbri, a northern tribe. As a result, Roman legions were reorganized to make them even more deadly.

Battle of Actium

In the sea near Greece, the forces of Augustus Caesar fought those of Anthony and Cleopatra in 31BCE. Some of Anthony's men deserted because they hated Cleopatra, and some of Cleopatra's men ran home to Egypt. Caesar won.

Fighting back

With its incredible power and wealth, Rome had plenty of enemies. Some brave souls defended their people against the powerful invader, while others attacked the mighty Empire itself.

Royal warrior

Boudicca was Queen of the Iceni, a Celtic tribe in Roman Britain. After her husband's death, the Romans stole her lands and robbed her people. In 60-61CE, her army destroyed a Roman legion and burned several Roman cities. When she was finally defeated, she killed herself by taking poison.

Nile queen

By joining forces with Julius Caesar, and later Mark Antony, Egyptian Queen Cleopatra hoped to gain power over Rome. But Caesar was murdered, and Antony killed himself. So, in 30BCE, Cleopatra ended her own life by letting a poisonous snake bite her.

Cleopatra

Enter the barbarians

The Goths were German barbarians (uncivilized people) – one tribe was called the Visigoths (west Goths). In 408CE, the Visigoth king, Alaric, marched his army to Rome and eventually conquered it. This was the beginning of the end of the Roman Empire.

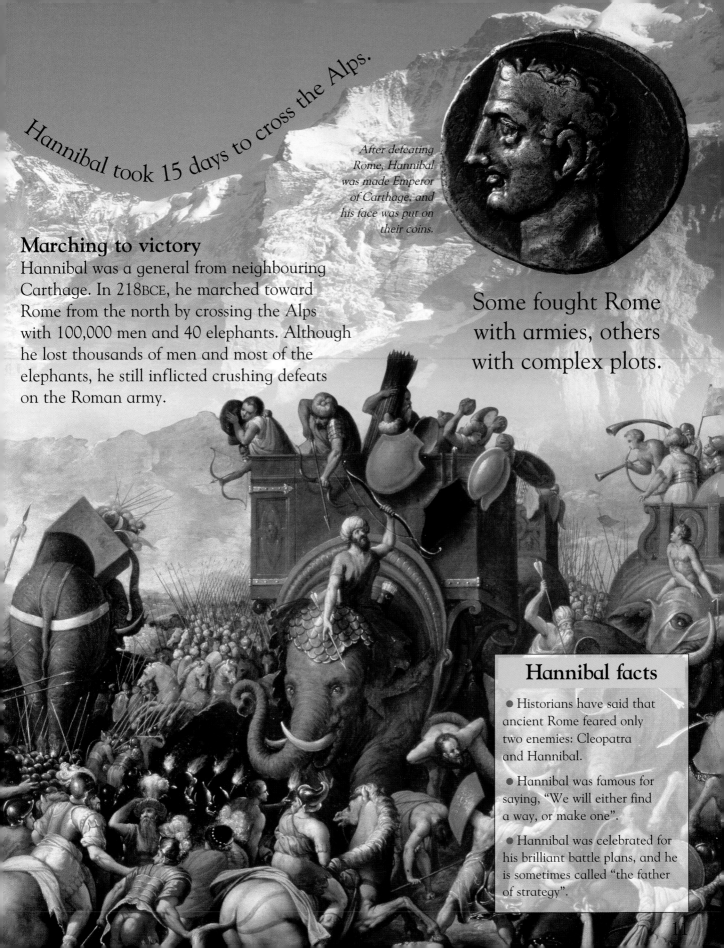

Hannibal took 15 days to cross the Alps.

After defeating Rome, Hannibal was made Emperor of Carthage, and his face was put on their coins.

Marching to victory

Hannibal was a general from neighbouring Carthage. In 218BCE, he marched toward Rome from the north by crossing the Alps with 100,000 men and 40 elephants. Although he lost thousands of men and most of the elephants, he still inflicted crushing defeats on the Roman army.

Some fought Rome with armies, others with complex plots.

Hannibal facts

● Historians have said that ancient Rome feared only two enemies: Cleopatra and Hannibal.

● Hannibal was famous for saying, "We will either find a way, or make one".

● Hannibal was celebrated for his brilliant battle plans, and he is sometimes called "the father of strategy".

The soldier's art

Rome's power came from her armies. These were called legions, and Roman soldiers were known as legionaries. Possibly the most successful armies of all time, they were made up of citizens who joined voluntarily, and were issued with fine uniforms and weapons.

Legionary

A soldier's helmet protected his face, head, and neck.

Where's the boss?

Legionaries carried huge wooden shields for protection. The handle in the middle had a meta cover on the outside, called [c] boss. This could be used to strike any enemy who got too close.

Soldiers would hang cups and a leather bottle of water or wine from their pack.

Shoulder packs

Legionaries were given large sacks to carry all their equipment and supplies – when they were full, these weighed up to 40kg (90lbs).

Spear

Weapons

Originally, legionaries carried thick spears designed for stabbing (far left). Later designs with a narrow point (left) were intended for throwing. These could pierce both shields and armour.

Standard bearer

Archer

Centurion

Soldiers helped each other to lace up.

Armour was made from metal strips fastened with leather, or leather and rope.

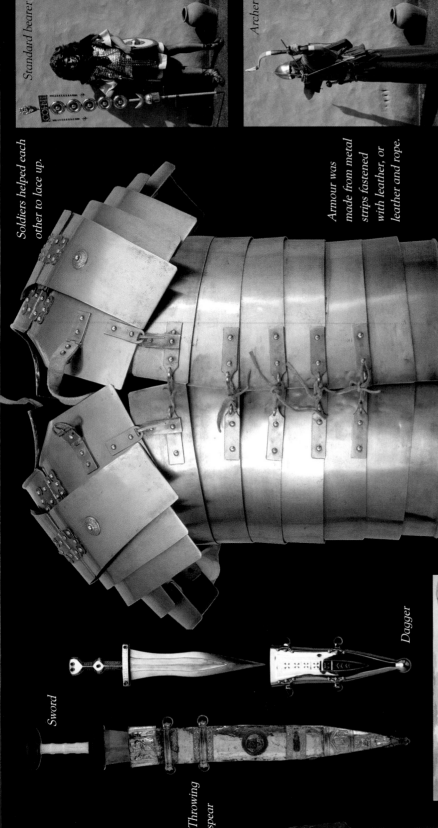

Just the job

Each legion had an emblem, or standard, carried by a standard bearer. Special soldiers called archers used bows and arrows. Each band of 100 men – a century – was led by a centurion.

Studded sandals

Sword

Throwing spear

Dagger

Making camp

When legionaries were on the march, they stopped at night to make camp. In about six hours, they could build a complex city.

The army in action

While the Roman army was led by its legions, backup was supplied by auxiliary regiments. These soldiers were not Roman citizens, but subjects from conquered lands, promised citizenship for their service. Together, the legions and the auxiliaries were almost unbeatable.

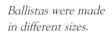

Ballistas were made in different sizes.

Throwing stones

One important weapon for Roman legionaries was the ballista – a type of catapult. This worked like a large crossbow to shoot arrows or stone balls.

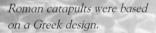

Roman catapults were based on a Greek design.

Left, right, left

Roman legionaries were highly organized and disciplined. They marched in step and moved as one unit, in response to blasts from a trumpet.

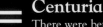 = **Centuria**
There were between 80 and 100 legionaries in a centuria.

2 Centuria

 = **Manipulus**
160-200 legionaries

On their horses

Although they were auxiliary troops, the cavalry (soldiers on horseback) were paid extra because they had to supply their own horses. They went ahead of the legions as guards and scouts. This carving is from the tomb of a Roman officer.

Tactical facts

● The Roman army could march up to 40km (25m) a day.

● We get our word "century" (100 years) from the Roman term *centuria*.

● Soldiers were paid very little, but they were given part of any land or valuables they helped to gain – the spoils of war.

Under siege

Auxiliary troops built siege towers – wheeled wooden structures that could be rolled up to enemy walls.

Wooden battering ram with iron head

With shields all around them, the legionaries formed an attacking formation called a "tortoise".

Cohort
480–600 legionaries

Legion
4800–6000 legionaries

A day in the life

In Roman towns and cities, street life was much like it is for us – people took walks, shopped, and stopped for a drink. Some everyday Roman activities, though, are less common today – like reading the future in fish guts.

Hub of activity

Most towns had a main square called the Forum. Statues of important people stood there, public notices were posted (newspapers didn't exist), and clubs and societies met.

Cloth merchants displayed lots of different textiles.

Thriving trade

Off the Forum were small streets of homes, and shops selling things like wine, shoes, spices, and food. There were workshops for blacksmiths, potters, glass blowers, and cloth makers, plus bars, restaurants, and offices.

Roads in Rome

Urban roads (paved, bricked, or left as dusty earth) were often dirty or flooded, so the paths on either side were raised. Huge stepping stones allowed people to cross from one side to the other.

Black as night

Towns and cities were very scary after dark. Romans lit their rooms, but the rough, dirty streets were almost pitch black, with no police to keep people safe.

Looking to the future

Romans visited fortune tellers for guidance about business, romance, or travel. Fortune tellers could "read" the future by watching birds, lightning, or other natural events. Sometimes they found answers by gutting a fish and examining its insides.

PUBLIC GATHERINGS

One convenience we share with the ancient Romans is the public toilet. Their public toilets, however, were considerably *more* public than ours. Instead of separate cubicles, Roman facilities consisted of rows of holes where people sat alongside their neighbours. Instead of paper, they used a sponge on the end of a stick.

Roman butchers used tools that looked just like ours.

Food was displayed appealingly to tempt customers.

Meet the emperors

Julius Caesar was a brilliant soldier who conquered many lands and peoples for the Empire. He declared himself absolute ruler in 44BCE. Soon after, he was murdered by a group of senators, who declared Rome to be a republic once again.

The first emperor

Caesar's adopted son, Octavian, was renamed Augustus Caesar. In 27BCE, he restored the republic in name only, but called himself "first citizen" and took absolute control. In fact, he was the first emperor.

Augustus means "the revered one".

Emperors wore a laurel wreath to symbolize their power.

"LITTLE BOOTS"

Rome's third emperor, Gaius (37-41CE), was nicknamed Caligula, which means "Little Boots". Caligula is best known as a madman – he thought he was a god, and threatened to make his favourite horse a consul. He acquired his affectionate nickname when he was a little boy – travelling with his army father, he liked to dress in a child-sized uniform.

Cruel leader

Septimus Severus (above) was declared emperor in 195BCE after a bloody civil war. A ruthless fighter and efficient leader (Severus is Latin for cruel), he may have inspired the name of the character Severus Snape in the *Harry Potter* books.

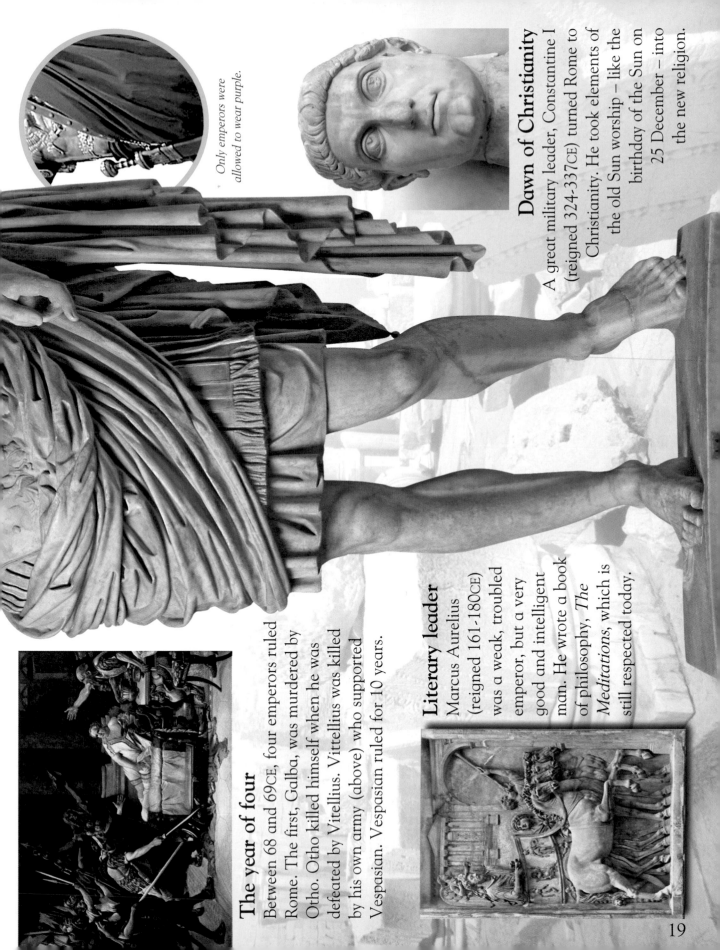

Only emperors were allowed to wear purple.

Dawn of Christianity

A great military leader, Constantine I (reigned 324-337CE) turned Rome to Christianity. He took elements of the old Sun worship – like the birthday of the Sun on 25 December – into the new religion.

The year of four

Between 68 and 69CE, four emperors ruled Rome. The first, Galba, was murdered by Otho. Otho killed himself when he was defeated by Vitellius. Vittellius was killed by his own army (above) who supported Vespasian. Vespasian ruled for 10 years.

Literary leader

Marcus Aurelius (reigned 161-180CE) was a weak, troubled emperor, but a very good and intelligent man. He wrote a book of philosophy, *The Meditations*, which is still respected today.

At home in Rome

The wealthiest Romans had fabulous houses called villas, which were decorated with fine paintings and mosaics. Ordinary families lived in simpler houses, but lots of poor people lived in shabby, multi-storey flats.

Tile art

The Romans loved mosaics – intricate decorations made with bits of tiles or glass. Mosaics can take the form of repeating designs, or lifelike pictures.

A single mosaic tile is called a tessera – the plural is tesserae.

The entrance to a grand villa might feature a mosaic dog to warn intruders that a ferocious beast was on guard!

All mod cons

Wealthy Romans were very comfortable at home – they had beautiful furnishings and lots of luxuries, such as running water and central heating.

Warmth came from hot water in under-floor pipes.

Windows were just holes in the wall, with no shutters to keep out the cold and rain.

Crowded spaces

Many people lived in multi-storey flats (often above shops) called *insulae*. These were cramped, dark, overcrowded, and often dangerous.

Insulae were mostly made of wood. They often caught fire or collapsed.

Open to the sky

Typical villas were built around a central courtyard (the *atrium)*, with a formal garden behind (the *peristylium*). Windows looked onto one of these – none faced the street.

Fast-food empire

Poor families had no space for cooking, so they bought ready-made meals from a Roman takeaway. These ruins show how the food was displayed.

Some people think of Roman interiors as pale and restrained. In fact, they were richly coloured, and adorned with beautiful pictures painted directly onto wet plaster.

At their leisure

Ancient Romans had no television, DVDs, or video games, but they loved going to the theatre, gladiator fights, and chariot races. They also enjoyed playing sports and dice games.

Winner takes all

One popular pastime was competing at board games that involved throwing dice. (Their dice were just like ours.) Romans loved to gamble, and would lay bets on most games and sports.

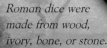

Roman dice were made from wood, ivory, bone, or stone.

Grace vs strength

The Romans adopted the sport of wrestling from the Greeks. Both Greeks and Romans allowed only upper-body contact, but the Romans valued strength and force over the skill and grace prized by the Greeks.

Like gladiators, charioteers were often ex-slaves.

Chariot teams each had their own colour – green, white, red, or blue.

Wheels on fire

At the racetrack, four teams of horses ran around an oval course. The tight turns at each end were the most dangerous part. Sometimes the chariot would fall, and the horses or the rider would be killed.

The ancient world's a stage

Romans enjoyed lots of performing arts, from music and dancing to plays. They particularly enjoyed mime – an informal mix of words, music, and dance that appeared in the street or at home.

Roman street musicians are shown in this mosaic, which adorns a Pompeiian villa.

Actors often wore masks to show whether their character was tragic or comic.

At the theatre

Admission to Roman theatres was free – everyone could watch formal plays, concerts, and pantomimes (which were a bit like masked ballets with one main performer). The audience sat in tiered seats that allowed everyone to see, and they could hear every whisper on the stage.

In Roman theatre, only men performed – women weren't allowed.

23

The Colosseum, the largest arena, could sit 50,000 people!

Roman arenas had lots of stairs, corridors, and entrances so people could get in and out easily.

Animals on display

Wild animals like lions, tigers, and bears fought both gladiators and other animals. Sometimes, they were placed in the ring simply to slaughter unarmed prisoners.

Thumbs UP!

A wounded gladiator could appeal to the emperor and crowd for mercy. If they put their thumbs up, the contest was stopped. If their thumbs went down, the gladiator was killed.

Killing for show

Romans, and their emperors, loved to watch people fight to the death in huge arenas. The men who put on this bloody show were prisoners or slaves trained in combat – the gladiators.

Sometimes the arena was flooded so gladiators could fight mock sea battles.

Wild animals were housed underneath the arena.

A gladiator who used a net to catch his opponent, and a long fork to kill him, was called a retiarius *(net man).*

Image is everything
Some gladiators took on specific roles – one who fought animals was called a *bestiarius* (animal man).

The floor of the arena would be covered in sand to soak up the blood.

Bath time

Roman bath houses were much more than places to wash. Here, at the end of the working day, lots of people would relax with friends, enjoy beauty and health treatments, exercise, and play sports.

Grand baths were adorned with marble, mosaics, and murals.

All change

Visitors undressed and left their clothes in changing rooms. Possessions were often stolen, though, so slaves were made to guard them. If you didn't have your own slave, you could hire one at the baths.

Some Roman baths, like those in the city of Bath in the UK, were filled from natural hot springs. These were thought to be very healthy.

All together now?

Experts think there were separate baths for men and women, or separate times for them to bathe, but we don't know this for sure.

Dealing with dirt

There was no soap in ancient Rome – bathers rubbed olive oil all over their body, then scraped it off with a curved, rounded blade called a *strigil*. Sometimes slaves would do this job for them.

Oil flask

Strigils were made from metal or bone.

This bath-house mosaic declares that "salvom lavisse" – "washing means health".

Health and fitness

As well as soaking in the bath, visitors might exercise, lift weights, and compete in athletic contests. Massages were popular, and these too might be done by a personal slave, or one provided by the bath house.

Roman work-out gear would look quite smart on a modern beach!

Palm branches were given as prizes.

To keep fit, Roman ladies lifted weights, threw the discus, and played ball games.

27

Keeping up appearances

Ancient Roman fashion didn't change quickly like it does today, but clothes and accessories served the same functions – they covered people up, kept them warm, and made them look nice.

Timeless style

With her softly curled hair and pretty gold jewellery, a wealthy Roman woman would not look out of place in the modern world.

This coloured-wax portrait comes from the case of a mummy from Roman-period Egypt.

Found in a grave, this ivory comb was more likely to be used for finding lice than for grooming.

The carving reads "Modestina, farewell".

Women's wear

Women wore simple straight tunics called *stolas* – often a short one layered on top of a long one. These could be white, but they were often coloured. Some ladies also wore a *palla* – a simple toga.

Baubles and bangles

Ordinary women wore jewellery made of amber, which was cheap and easily available. Wealthy women wore gold and precious stones.

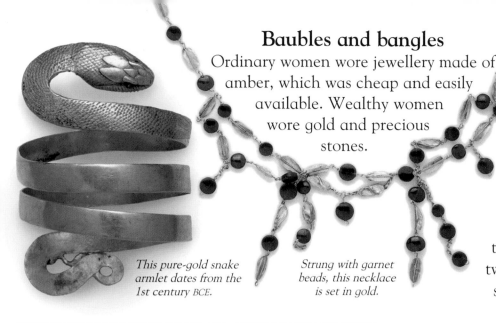

Many women had their ears pierced for earrings.

This pure-gold snake armlet dates from the 1st century BCE.

Strung with garnet beads, this necklace is set in gold.

Grooming set

Found in Roman ruins in the UK, these tools include tweezers, a pumice stone for smoothing rough skin, and an earwax scoop.

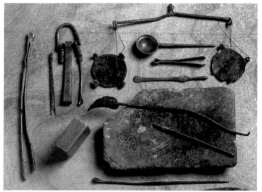

Peasants   Nobleman   Temple officials   Citizen

Men's department

Only Roman citizens wore togas, and then just on formal occasions – historians think these were half-circle shapes (usually wool) about 3m (10ft) long by 2m (6ft 6in) wide. Ordinarily, everybody wore knee-length sleeveless tunics.

Senators wore togas with a purple border. This colour, which came only from a rare sea snail, still represents status today.

Tucking in

Like us, the Romans had three meals a day. Breakfast and lunch were small and quick – maybe just bread and fruit. The main meal of the day was a large, leisurely dinner. Eaten in late afternoon, it was an important social event for family and friends.

phew! eeuw!

Garum factories were far from towns because of the stink.

Smelly sauce
Because food went bad very quickly, people used sauce to disguise its taste. The favourite was *garum*, made from fish (guts, blood, and all), salt, and herbs – all mashed in a pot and left to rot.

Herbs

Salt

Fish

Fish guts

Ground meat rolled in breadcrumbs

Finger food
People ate with their fingers or with spoons – there were knives in the kitchen, but not on the table. Food was served in small pieces, and arranged in bowls – diners helped themselves.

Fare and fowl
Romans ate lots of things we enjoy – bread and pastry, fish and shellfish, cheese, poultry and meat, eggs, vegetables, and fruit. But they had some strange favourites too, such as lark tongue and peacock brains.

Food facts

- Banquets had so many courses, diners would make themselves sick so they could keep eating!

- Dinner guests took their own napkin, and used it for wrapping leftovers to take home.

- Romans preserved food by pickling, drying, smoking, and salting. This didn't always work, though, so food poisoning was probably common.

Roman kitchens

Food was cooked in pots on flat metal stands, or hung from chains over an open fire. Smoke escaped through a small hole in the ceiling or wall. Bread and pastry were cooked in round ovens, and sometimes poor families shared one large, communal oven.

Strainer

Bowl

Knife

Serving slave

Relax and enjoy

Family meals were eaten sitting around a table, but at banquets (attended only by men), diners lounged diagonally on couches. These were placed around three sides of a table, giving access for slaves to bring food and take dishes away.

Growing up in Rome

In ancient Rome, children looked (and were expected to behave) just like grown-ups, only smaller. They were considered the property of their father, who sometimes kept control of his daughters even after they married.

In this stone sculpture, children are shown as tiny adults. This is just how Roman society saw them.

Fun and games

Roman children played with some of the same toys you do, like marbles, balls, hoops, model animals, and toy vehicles (chariots, not racing cars!).

Cuddly toy

Little girls have always played with dolls. Preserved in the dry soil of Egypt, this simple rag figure is well worn, as if a Roman child loved it very much.

Do you play with marbles that look like these Roman ones?

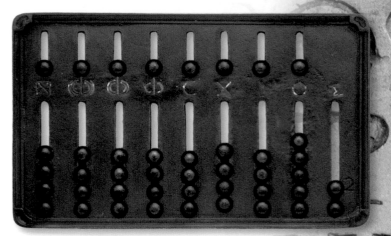

Home zoo

Family pets were kept mainly for children. Romans kept dogs and caged birds, and some people had monkeys, which they taught to do tricks.

Out for the count

Instead of a calculator, Roman children used a tool called an abacus to work out their sums. This one has a surprisingly sleek, modern look.

Some Roman letters looked just like the ones used in many modern languages.

Wax tablet

School days

Some children had tutors at home, but many went to school for their lessons (below). They scratched letters on a wax tablet (left) instead of writing on paper. Boys were given much more education than girls, who learned how to run a home.

Stone sculpture of school

Slave labour

In ancient Rome, people could own other people – adults and children – like they owned animals and furniture, and they could sell or rent them out in the same way. The people who were owned were called slaves.

Slaves for sale

Roman citizens bought slaves in slave markets. They were displayed wearing very few clothes so people could see how strong and healthy they were.

Care and treatment

Many slaves had to wear an identity bracelet. Some were chained, or even branded with a hot iron. Most were treated well though, since healthy slaves could do more work!

Identity bracelet

Child slaves

Children of slaves often became slaves too, especially if their parents worked in a large household, which they could join. Sometimes, people who weren't slaves were so poor, they sold their own children as slaves.

Hard labour

Slaves did most of the work in every area of Roman life. Some jobs, like road building (right), mining, and farming, were very hard and tiring.

Home work

Domestic work was easier – slaves were often part of the family. They not only did cooking, cleaning, and childcare, they also dressed their owners, did their hair, and carried them through the streets on a handled chair called a litter.

Female slaves dressing their mistress.

Popular gladiators could become rich and famous.

Freed slaves could not vote, but their children could.

All the slaves in the town of Hesta were freed by this bronze decree in 3BCE.

Finding freedom

If they raised the money, slaves could buy their freedom. Some did this by taking on the dangerous life of a gladiator or charioteer. Sometimes slaves were freed by their masters.

Country living

In the Roman countryside, there were four basic types of dwelling – the small peasant farm, the grand country house, the big working farm, and the great estate that combined villa and farm.

Olive oil was burned in special lamps to provide light.

Villa courtyards were large and elegant.

Country retreats

In the Roman Empire, as in many modern countries, wealthy city dwellers kept a country home where they could escape. These villas were much like grand city houses, with gardens and pools.

Precious oil

Olives were a vital crop in ancient Rome. They were a staple food, and they were also pressed to make olive oil, consumed at home and exported widely.

Country facts

- The Romans grew carrots, onions, cucumbers, radishes, figs, cherries, and plums.

- To pick olives, workers shook the tree branches until the fruit fell off – they still do.

- Farmers kept cattle for dairy products, meat, and leather.

Grapes for wine

Grapes were another major crop – some were eaten as fruit, but most were pressed to make wine. The Romans drank wine in large quantities (usually watered down), and shipped it across the Empire.

Grapes were picked by hand and put in a large vat. Workers then stamped on them to make juice.

Life on the land

Not all farming was done by rich families who owned lots of land and slaves. Some produce came from peasants who tended very small farms, and grew only one or two crops.

This 3rd-century mosaic shows farmers ploughing in Gaul (Roman France).

Thrill of the hunt

Throughout history, country people have hunted wild animals. Ancient Romans hunted on foot and on horseback – this party used dogs and spears to flush out a wild boar.

Gods and worship

Many religions honour a single, central figure (like Buddha, God, or Allah), but the Romans had lots of gods. These could even change from one century, or part of the Empire, to another. Some emperors were made gods when they died.

Neptune was the god of the sea.

Jupiter was the chief Roman god and protector of the Empire.

Choose your god

In ancient Rome, there were hundreds of gods, goddesses, half-gods, and spirits. Many were adopted from the Greeks or the Etruscans. New gods were added all the time from conquered lands such as Persia and Turkey.

Diana was the goddess of the Moon and of hunting.

A dedication to Bacchus, the Roman god of wine and drunkenness, interpreted in a Victorian painting.

Roman worship

Roman towns and cities had many temples, each dedicated to a different god – people would make offerings to the one they needed at the time. Roman religion did not set down specific rules, or standards of behaviour.

Temples had columns, steps, and a triangular shape called a pediment.

Home help

In each home, offerings were made at a small shrine dedicated to domestic gods and spirits. A man's personal protective spirit was a *genus*, and a woman's was a *juno*.

The spirit of a family's ancestors was a lar.

Early Christian mosaic of the Last Supper.

The coming of Christ

When Jesus first became popular, he was seen as a threat to law and order, and killed by the Roman authorities. Christianity was declared illegal, but its popularity spread. By the 4th century, encouraged by Emperor Constantine I, it became Rome's official religion.

Trade and transport

When goods travelled by road, they were loaded onto simple wagons drawn by horses or mules.

One of the reasons the Roman Empire was so prosperous was its incredibly efficient transport systems. Romans were able to bring in a wide range of goods from the far corners of the Empire, and send their own products abroad to be sold.

Roman ports featured elegant architecture and landscaping intended to impress visiting merchants and traders.

Wine and olive oil were transported in curved pottery jars called amphorae.

Over the waves

Barges and sailing ships were used to transport bulky goods to and from far-away provinces such as Africa and Britain. To protect them from pirates, the Roman navy patrolled the seas.

Stone model of a ship transporting wine in Germania, modern-day Germany

The exotic east

From the far east, along the trail known as the silk road, came silk from China, perfumes from Arabia (the middle east), and cotton, precious stones, and dyes such as indigo from India.

Selling spices

Fragrant spices like saffron, ginger, and nutmeg were brought in from Arabia and India.

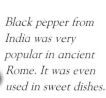

Black pepper from India was very popular in ancient Rome. It was even used in sweet dishes.

British metal

In Britain, the Romans mined precious metals like gold and silver, which they made into coins and jewellery. They also dug tin, lead, and iron from the ground.

Egypt was known as Rome's bread basket.

African harvest

Egypt made an important contribution to the Empire. It supplied wheat to make bread, and papyrus (made from a wetland plant), which the Romans used as paper.

Northern bounty

Then, as now, most of the world's amber (fossilized tree resin) came from Eastern Europe. The Romans used it to make jewellery, which they wore to prevent bad luck.

The Empire lives on

Roman architecture and engineering were so brilliant that lots of their buildings and monuments are still standing today. Some are in ruins, but others look just as beautiful as they did thousands of years ago.

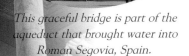

This graceful bridge is part of the aqueduct that brought water into Roman Segovia, Spain.

Baths of Bath

In Britain, the Romans built a city they named *Aquae Sulis* (waters of Sulis, goddess of wisdom). The city, now called Bath, and its baths are still operating today.

African remains

The city of Leptis Magna in Libya is one of the most stunning Roman ruins in the Mediterranean. Its theatre attracts thousands of visitors every year.

The Roman Library at Ephesus, Turkey, once held nearly 12,000 scrolls (their equivalent of books). The main reading room faces east to catch the morning sun.

Modern arch

For centuries, the arch of Septimus Severus in Rome's forum was buried in rubble. Then, in the late 1700s, it was excavated along with the rest of the Forum.

Going strong

The most complete Roman building still in existence is the Pantheon, a domed temple in Rome itself. Built by Hadrian in 125CE, it became a church in 609, and it still serves as a church today.

Lots of famous people like the painter Raphael are buried in the Pantheon.

Until the 1400s, this was the biggest dome in the world.

CONCRETE ACHIEVEMENTS

One reason Roman structures lasted so long was their solid concrete construction. Although similar materials were used by earlier cultures, the Romans developed their superior concrete – a mixture of lime mortar, sand, stones, and water – to replace stone. Nothing better was invented until the 18th century.

The Romans gave us...

The ancient Romans lived a long, long time ago, so it's easy to think their civilization was basic and primitive. But they were brilliant inventors, engineers, and architects, and they left us a rich legacy of knowledge and technology.

Water, water
Roman plumbing was more advanced than any system in the world until the 1800s. Aqueducts brought water into towns and cities for public baths, fountains, and toilets.

This aqueduct in France was built without mortar. The stones were cut precisely to fit.

A modern world

In ancient Rome, you would have seen:

- one-way systems
- fast-food stalls
- graffiti
- bars
- running water
- pop (gladiator) celebrities
- double glazing

Warm and cosy

In Rome, public baths and the homes of wealthy people were kept warm with complex central-heating systems. These were powered by underground furnaces tended by slaves.

Heat passed under the floor and through spaces in the walls. This warmed the rooms but didn't fill them with smoke.

Month by month

The Romans named the months after their gods and emperors. In many languages, we still use their names today – March, for example, is named for the war god Mars.

The month of August was named after Augustus Caesar.

Word power

We still read and enjoy Roman stories, plays, and poetry. Writers like Virgil (above centre) have provided inspiration and enjoyment for thousands of years.

The Romans replaced dirt tracks with roads that had a strong foundation and several layers.

Roads ahead

The roads we use today are built to a Roman design. Their engineers were the first to make roads domed in the middle, so rainwater could drain away. In countries that were once part of the Empire, many routes follow ancient Roman roads.

Glossary

Here are some words that are useful to know when
you're learning about ancient Rome.

amphitheatre an oval arena,
usually in the open air, where
gladiators fought. The
Colosseum is an amphitheatre.

aqueduct a special channel
(either raised up or buried
underground) that carried water
into Roman towns and cities.

atrium the central hall of a
Roman house, which was open
to the sky. Most rooms opened
off the atrium.

barbarians a term used to
describe unfamiliar people who
were thought to be coarse,
wild, and uncultured.

catapult machine used during a
siege to hurl stones and darts at
or over enemy walls.

century a company of about
100 men in the Roman army.
Each century was led by an
officer called a centurion.

circus a round or oval stadium
where chariot races were held.

citizen a free man as opposed
to a slave. Citizens had many
rights and privileges, including
the right to vote. (*see also* slave)

cohort sub-division of the
Roman army. Each cohort
contained three manipuli.
(*see also* manipulus)

couch backless seat, sometimes
with ornate ends, on which
Romans relaxed at home, and
reclined to eat formal meals.

emperor the absolute ruler
of an empire – "emperor" was
a higher rank than "king".
Augustus Caesar became the
first Roman emperor in 27BCE.

forum the main market square,
surrounded by public buildings,
in a Roman town or city. Public
business, as well as trade, was
carried on there.

garum a strong-tasting sauce
made from rotten fish, salt, and
flavourings.

gladiator a trained fighter
(usually a slave or a prisoner)
who battled other gladiators
– or wild animals – to the death
in public contests.

laurel wreath circle woven from the leaves of a kind of bay plant, to be worn on the head of a leader. A laurel wreath symbolized power.

legion main division of the Roman army. Each legion contained ten cohorts. (*see also* cohort)

legionary a soldier in the Roman army. (*see also* legion)

manipulus an army unit consisting of two centuria. (*see also* century)

mosaic decorated wall or floor made from small pieces of glass, stone, or tile cemented into position. Mosaics can make a picture or a pattern. (*see also* tesserae)

papyrus an Egyptian water reed whose stem was pressed and dried to make the paper-like sheets Romans wrote on.

peristyle garden surrounded by columns, and often found behind a grand Roman house.

province a Roman territory that was far from the city. The people who already lived there were called "provincials".

relief a carved or moulded image that stands out from its background.

republic a state where power is held by the people, or their representatives, through voting, rather than by a king or an emperor.

slave a man, woman, or child who is owned by another person as property, usually to do work of some kind.

standard a flag or small statue that is the emblem of an organization, often an army or military unit.

tesserae the small pieces of stone, glass, or tile that are used to make a mosaic. (*see also* mosaic)

toga formal garment worn by male citizens. It consisted of a length of fabric, usually white, wrapped around the body and draped over one shoulder.

tunic simple top, tied at the waist and reaching the knees.

villa luxurious house belonging to a wealthy Roman family.

Index

Acknowledgements

Dorling Kindersley would like to thank:
Andy Cooke for his original illustrations; Penny Smith, Joe Harris, Fleur Star, Nellie Greenwood, and Carrie Love for editorial help; Gemma Fletcher, Mary Sandberg, and Sonia Moore for design assistance.

Picture credits

The publisher would like to thank the following for their kind permission to reproduce their photographs:
Key: a-above; b-below/bottom; c-centre; l-left; r-right; t-top

Alamy Images: Atmosphere Picture Library 42cr; Mary Evans Picture Library 24br; Scott Hortop Travel 42tl; imagebroker 40t; INTERFOTO Pressebildagentur 20tr; Brenda Kean 16l, 42br; Lebrecht Music and Arts Photo LibraryB3HYF 31bl; Liquid Light 27cl; The London Art Archive 5cb, 9cla, 9tr; David Lyons 8tr; Picture Contact 12t, 13tc, 13tl, 13tr; David Stares 1; Jack Sullivan 14c; Jochen Tack 14br; Claudia Witry 30cl; **Ancient Art & Architecture Collection:** C.M. Dixon 23tr, 34c; Prisma 36b, 37tc; **The Art Archive:** Alfredo Dagli Orti/Museo Civico Udine 22c; Gianni Dagli Orti 26c; Museo della Civilta Romana Rome / Gianni Dagli Orti 32bl, 35bl; Alfredo Dagli Orti/National Archaeological Museum Chieti 8tl; Dagli Orti/Bardo Museum, Tunis 22tl; Private Collection/Eileen Tweedy 27tr; **The Bridgeman Art Library:** 39br; Ancient Art & Architecture 5t; Museo Archeologico Nazionale, Naples 17tr; Museo della Civilta Romana, Rome, Italy / Roger-Viollet, Paris545 17bl; Museo Ostiense, Ostia Antica, Rome, Italy/Roger-Viollet, Paris 17br; The Stapleton Collection/Private Collection 13br; **Corbis:** 38t; Alinari Archives 22tr; Alinari Archives/Mauro Magliani 24bl; Bettmann 10b, 10c, 18tl, 18tr,

34tl; Jonathan Blair 17cl; The Art Archive 25b, 32tl; Elio Ciol 41br; Gianni Dagli Orti 45cl; Araldo de Luca 2t, 14l, 16bc, 18-19c, 23tl, 26 (background), 28r, 29tl, 33r, 35cl, 38-39c, 48c; The Gallery Collection 20-21b, 21r, 38b, 38tr; Robert Harding World Imagery 44; John Harper 19; Hoberman Collection 41cr; Image Source 18bl; Mimmo Jodice 21br, 21c, 21tr, 39cr, 40cl, 45bl; Richard T. Nowitz 36r; PhotoCuisine 41cl; Vittoriano Rastelli 48; Redlink 41t; Ron Chapple 4tl, 24-25; Leonard de Selva 27b; Stapleton Collection 6c; Roger Wood 28tl, 42c, 45tr, 46-47; Zefa 10-11t; **DK Images:** Christi Graham and Nick Nicholls (c) The British Museum 5cra, 28c, 29tc, 29tr, 31tl, 31tr, 32tr; John Chase/The Museum of London 31tc; Peter Hayman (c) The British Museum 40cr; The British Museum 27tl; Tim Ridley 31br; British Museum, London 32br; Courtesy of the Science Museum, London/Dave King 33tc; **Getty Images:** 18br; Bridgeman Art Library 5bl, 7cr, 9clb, 19br, 33b, 34-35, 35tr, 37cl, 38cl, 40b; MedioImages 5br; Adam Crowley 3, 42l; DEA Picture Library 41bl; Michael Dunning 43; Gallo Images 18; Sylvain Grandadam 4b; Hulton Archive 4tr; Wolfgang Kaehler 7bl; Richard Nowitz 17tl; R H Productions 2l; Chris Rennie 23; Taxi/Jon Eisberg 26b; **Steve Haasis** (www.ancientvine.com): 8b, 14cl, 16tr, 39t; Chris Haigh: 22b; **Heritage Images:** Ann Ronan Picture Library 15tl; **iStockphoto.com:** Sue Colvil 8-9t, 9br; lilly3 30cra; Malcolm Romain 19tl; **Mary Laskin:** 30b; **Mary Evans Picture Library:** 28bl, 29bl; **Photolibrary:** Jochen Tack 6b; **Reuters:** Dario Pignatelli 35br; Photo Scala, Florence: Bardo Museum 33tl; Courtesy Ministero Beni e Att. Culurali 34cl, 37br; **Science Photo Library:** Robert Brook 30crb; **St Albans Museums:** 29cr, 33cl; **SuperStock:** 11b; Dawn Wagner: 20bc

Jacket images: Front: Corbis: Alinari Archives/Mauro Magliani c (main image), t. **Back: DK Images:** The British Museum br, tc; **Getty Images:** Egyptian cra

All other images © Dorling Kindersley

For further information see: www.dkimages.com